THE IMPOSSIBLE
MADE
POSSIBLE

An Interactive Devotional Journey
Toward Radical Forgiveness

MIKE NOVOTNY

Published by Straight Talk Books
P.O. Box 301, Milwaukee, WI 53201
800.661.3311 · timeofgrace.org

Printed in the United States of America
ISBN: 978-1-949488-41-8

He does not treat us as our sins deserve
or repay us according to our iniquities.
For as high as the heavens are above the earth,
so great is his love for those who fear him;
as far as the east is from the west,
so far has he removed our transgressions from us.
As a father has compassion on his children,
so the Lord has compassion on those who fear him;
for he knows how we are formed,
he remembers that we are dust.

PSALM 103:10-14

INTRODUCTION

Years ago I got into a rather unloving exchange with a fellow Christian. The tension had been growing for months, so we met face-to-face to figure it out. As we talked about what God would want us to do—just love—she closed her eyes and gave a slow nod: "I know . . . I know . . ." I sighed, because I knew exactly how she felt. As a Christian, I wanted to let it go and choose to love her as the Bible commands. But it can be so hard to get the truth of the Word into the emotions of your heart, the thoughts of your mind, and the words of your lips.

Have you felt that too?

If so, Jesus wants to help. That's why he taught us to pray, **"Father . . . we also forgive everyone who sins against us"** (Luke 11:2,4). Our Savior knew how hard forgiveness would be, so he directed us to the source of supernatural power. When you feel like you can't, talk to the God who always can!

But look at what Jesus said first: **"Forgive us *our sins*, for we also forgive everyone who sins against us"** (Luke 11:4). "First, Father, forgive us our sins. Forgive my sins." Forgiveness starts not with you forgiving them but with God forgiving you. And he has! And he is! And he will!

That's what this devotional journal is all about. I want to take you through the steps of forgiving those who sin against you. I want to show you God's way. I want to show you that looking to him in prayer for help is absolutely necessary because it's not easy to forgive.

Throughout these pages, I'm going to use the analogy of stones—these are the sins other people throw at you. They're the stones you can choose either to pick up and throw back in an angry attempt at getting them back. Or they're the stones you can choose to leave alone as you forgive and get past the wrongdoing.

Let's walk through these steps together, and I pray that when at times you find forgiving seems impossible, that you remember to pray to your supremely capable and shockingly forgiving Father who's forgiven you.

Pastor Mike

**In [Jesus] we have
redemption through his blood,
the forgiveness of sins.**

EPHESIANS 1:7

WHERE FORGIVENESS BEGINS

Have you ever seen the musical (or read the book) *Les Misérables?* It is, in part, about a convict named Jean Valjean who refuses to forgive the legal system that sinned against him, leaving him broke and broken. In his bitterness, Valjean decides to steal some silver candlesticks from a kind priest who showed him only love. The police catch him and are ready to bring the hammer of justice down on his head, but the priest defends Valjean, claiming the candlesticks were a gift. Stunned, Valjean stares as the priest draws close to his ear and says in a low voice, "Jean Valjean, my brother, you no longer belong to evil, but to good. . . . I withdraw [your soul] from black thoughts and . . . I give it to God." I won't ruin the rest of the story, but I will tell you that this absurd forgiveness changes Jean Valjean.

It changes us too. Like that priest, Jesus has shown us grace. When justice would have locked us up in hell, far from God, Jesus leans in close and whispers, "I forgive you. I bled to buy you back and give you to God." The apostle Paul writes, **"In [Jesus] we have redemption through his blood, the forgiveness of sins"** (Ephesians 1:7).

Meditate deeply upon that gospel truth. God, for the rest of your life, will never get you back. He will never treat you as your sins deserve. He will always love you.

That kind of forgiveness never leaves a soul the same. Just ask Jean Valjean.

MORE ON THE TOPIC . . .

"When we come to church and pray the Lord's Prayer, when we sit down at the end of a hard day, before we get to the other people we need to forgive, we just start with us and God. And when we realize that Jesus is just like that priest with Jean Valjean, he is so good to us and still, we sin against him and yet, he's still so good to us. Even the times we knew better and we've taken from him, he says, 'No, no, no, I withdraw your soul from punishment, from prison, from hell, and give it to God. I bless you in ways that you don't deserve. I will not treat you as your sins deserve to be treated. Instead, I will love and give and listen and be there for you.' And when that thought sinks deep into your heart that God—God!—would do that for a person like me, then I'm ready to look at him or her and to forgive. Then I'm ready to glance at the biggest stones of my past and let them alone. How could I throw that at him if God didn't throw the stone at me?"

From *Time of Grace* series *Forgiveness Is Offensive*, episode: "When Forgiving Feels Impossible"

DIG DEEPER

Have you ever experienced a time when someone forgave you even though you didn't deserve it at all, even though you weren't even particularly repentant? Describe it here.

Is there someone in your life whom you could forgive in this way?

With whom does forgiveness begin?

Read Psalm 103:10-12. Break these verses down and describe God's forgiveness for you.

Why won't God ever treat you as your sin deserves?

What stones were thrown at you today?

How did you handle those stones?

Write a prayer thanking God for his unending mercy and forgiveness.

For I will forgive their wickedness and will remember their sins no more.

JEREMIAH 31:34

WHAT TO DO WHEN SOMEONE SINS AGAINST YOU
Part 1

When someone's sin hits you like a stone, hurting you deeply, there are four things you can do. First—You can try to forget. People say, "You need to forgive *and* forget." That sounds like a nice Pinterest post, but is that idea biblical?

I searched the Bible and learned that the word *forget* is used 64 times. Guess how many have to do with forgetting about someone else's sin? Zero. In fact, "forgive and forget" could be a guilt-inducing, danger-producing way to live. If you have to forget to truly forgive, how many of us could ever do it? How could we forget the source of those scars that came from our ex's abuse, our dad's addiction, or the cruel words from some mean classmates?

In addition, if we forgot every sin, how would we know who are the fools and wicked souls whom God warns us about in Proverbs and in Paul's letters?

No, the truth is that you can forgive, even if their sin is impossible to forget. (More on this in the days to come.)

Today, as you try to forgive what you can't forget, remember the unique forgiveness of God: **"I will forgive their wickedness and will remember their sins no more"** (Jeremiah 31:34). This is the one-sided promise that comes to us at the cross and at the cost of Jesus' blood.

The all-knowing God is certainly not forgetful, but (thank you, Jesus!) he chooses to remember our sins no more.

MORE ON THE TOPIC . . .

"The people who've thrown stones at us—should we treat them like they deserve to be treated? The Bible's answer is no. Should we carry along this list of grudges and hurts and hang-ups in our hearts to get them back? The Bible's answer is no. But does that mean that if you still can remember the things that have been done to you that you haven't truly forgiven? Now the answer to that question would be no. In fact, I would contend this: Do you know the person who really, really, really wants you to try to forgive and forget? The devil. Because if you think deep in your soul that to forgive someone means you have to forget that it happened, guess who's going to win? When you get thumped by a terrible sin and you're bruised and you're scarred, time might heal that wound but the scar still remains and the stone sits at your feet. How do you just forget that? The devil would love for you to believe this guilt-inducing lie: If you haven't forgotten it, you haven't forgiven it. He wants you to believe that you must not be a forgiving person, which means maybe that you're not even a Christian. So forgive and forget? The answer's no. God doesn't demand that; he doesn't command that. Don't treat people like they deserve to be treated, but you can still remember and still forgive."

From *Time of Grace* series *Forgiveness Is Offensive*, episode: "You Must Forgive EVERY Day"

DIG DEEPER

Can you think of a particular stone that was thrown at you recently or in the past that has been hard to forget? Write about it here.

Think of a time when you were tempted to treat someone as they deserved for wronging you. How did that turn out for you?

When God says, "I will remember their sins no more," what does that mean? Does God really "forget"?

You are completely forgiven of all your wrongdoing through Jesus. How does that kind of forgiveness change you?

List some ways that you can leave the previously mentioned stone alone and forgive the person who threw it.

What other stones were thrown at you today?

How did you handle those stones?

Write a prayer asking God for the strength and humility to forgive even when you can't forget.

Do not repay evil with evil or insult with insult.

1 PETER 3:9

———

You have heard that it was said,
"Love your neighbor and hate your enemy."
But I tell you, love your enemies.

MATTHEW 5:43,44

WHAT TO DO WHEN SOMEONE SINS AGAINST YOU
Part 2

When someone's sin hits you like a stone, hurting you deeply, there are four things you can do. Here's the second—You can get them back. You can pick up the stone and throw, making them hurt just like they hurt you. That might feel like the right thing to do, but vengeance won't work.

Just ask Samson and the Philistines. In the Bible book called Judges, the Philistines threatened to kill Samson's wife, so Samson killed 30 of their men. So the Philistines killed Samson's girl and her dad. So Samson picked up that stone and covered the rocks with Philistine blood. So the Philistines picked up that stone, bribed Samson's girlfriend, captured their rival, and gouged out his eyes. So blind Samson picked up that stone and tore down the temple where the Philistines gathered to mock him. They died. He died. Everyone died. The end. The score was never settled.

You won't settle the score either. If you make them hurt, it won't help. Hearts don't heal like that. In fact, once your stone is thrown, they'll pick it up and throw it right back. Perhaps that's why Jesus taught: **"You have heard that it was said, 'Love your neighbor and hate your enemy.' But I tell you, love your enemies"** (Matthew 5:43,44).

If you want more pain, then make them pay. If you prefer peace, choose the path of forgiveness. Just like Jesus chose to forgive you and give you peace with our Father above.

MORE ON THE TOPIC . . .

"Good ol' karma. Payback. Vengeance. You don't need a YouTube tutorial to know how to do it. As soon as that sin-stone hits you, it drops to the ground, which means you just have to lean over for a weapon to throw back. Every one of you who grew up with a little brother or an older sister knows exactly how this works, right? Mom asked, 'Why did you punch your sister?' And you said, 'Because she punched me first,' right? That's what you do, right? You've got to settle the score; justice has to be carried out. . . . It's instinctual; you don't even have to think about it. When someone treats you in a wrong way, the sinful part of your heart just wants to reach down, grab that stone, and throw it right back. But God would say to you today, 'Don't.' Not just because it's not right but because it won't work. . . . You know what happens—back and forth and back and forth and back and forth until there are grudges and divisions and animosity and rivalries. When we choose to take justice into our hands instead of leaving it to God, it never works out. And so as natural and as instinctual as it might be, God doesn't want us to touch that stone because he knows what's about to happen."

From *Time of Grace* series *Forgiveness Is Offensive*, episode: "You Must Forgive EVERY Day"

DIG DEEPER

Have you ever chosen the path of payback when someone has wronged you? What happened?

Many books and movies have been written around the topic of settling a score. Can you list at least three?

Did any of those books or movies end with the wronged standing by and forgiving the other? Why is that an unnatural reaction to wrongdoing for us?

Why do you think the devil loves to keep you remembering someone else's wrong?

Loving your enemies sounds hard. Can you think of some practical ways you can do exactly that as you strive to live a life of forgiveness?

What stones were thrown at you today?

How did you handle those stones?

Write a prayer asking God to help you love all people—
even those who've wronged you.

**See to it that . . . no bitter root grows up
to cause trouble and defile many.**

HEBREWS 12:15

WHAT TO DO WHEN SOMEONE SINS AGAINST YOU
Part 3

When someone's sin hits you like a stone, hurting you deeply, there are four things you can do. Here's the third—Get bitter. Bitterness is when you pick up the sin that hurt you and hold on to it. You don't throw it back in vengeance but instead curl your fingers around its edges, going through the ugly event in your mind, retelling the story of your pain to anyone who will listen. But that bitterness will destroy you.

My first job involved hours and hours (and hours) of Weedwhacking at a golf course. I'd gas up the tank, grip the handle, and pull the trigger until the fuel ran out. But by the time my shift was done, my hands could barely move. I had held on to the Weedwhacker's handle for so long that my fingers were stuck in that position.

Bitterness is like that. The longer you hold on to that stone, the harder it is to let it go. Hebrews warns, **"See to it that . . . no bitter root grows up to cause trouble and defile many"** (12:15). Bitterness is a root that produces toxic fruit. It leaves you stuck—troubled and defiled. Getting bitter never makes it better.

So, friend, let that stone alone. Pry open your fingers with prayer, and let the past go. Ask the Holy Spirit for help (he wants to!). Ask your Father to remind you of your own forgiveness. Ask Jesus to help you love your enemies.

Just like he loved you when you were his enemy.

MORE ON THE TOPIC . . .

"Bitterness is when you grab that stone and hold on to it.
. . . But friends, I want to warn you. Holding on to sin for
another day will just make it harder to let go tomorrow.
. . . When we refuse to give up memory to God, we hold
on to it. And the longer we hold on to it, the harder it is
to let go of it. And God sees what happens, that when our
hands aren't open, it's not just the person who threw
the stone that hurts us. It's that we become incapable
of joining hands with anyone. Our hands aren't free; our
hearts aren't clean enough to pray and to bless, to offer
grace and mercy. Maybe it's why in the book of Hebrews
we find these words. God says, 'See to it that . . . no bitter
root grows up to cause trouble and defile many' (12:15).
A bitter root. And every day that root gets stronger and
produces toxic fruit that will ruin your relationships and
ruin your life. So our heavenly Father in love says that
you don't have to forget it, but he doesn't want you to
touch that stone. Don't grab it to pay someone back;
don't grab it to hold on to it or stew about it."

**From *Time of Grace* series *Forgiveness Is Offensive*,
episode: "You Must Forgive EVERY Day"**

DIG DEEPER

Bitterness is when you pick up a stone that someone's thrown at you and hold on to it and let it fester in your mind and dwell on it. You don't let it go. How do you think you'll feel if you hold on to that stone? Will you feel better in the end? Why or why not?

Bitterness toward others when they've wronged you can lead to a bitter outlook on life overall. Read Ephesians 4:31,32. What does God say is a better way?

Read the parable of the unmerciful servant in Matthew 18:21-35. Who is God in this parable? How much did he forgive? Who are you and I in this parable when we hold on to bitterness toward someone else's wrong?

We have been forgiven so much! What does that mean for you in your relationships with others?

What stones were thrown at you today?

How did you handle those stones?

Are you currently holding any grudges or bitterness toward someone? Remind yourself of how often Jesus has forgiven you. Write a prayer for a heart of forgiveness.

**Repay evil with blessing,
because to this you were called
so that you may inherit a blessing.**

1 PETER 3:9

WHAT TO DO WHEN SOMEONE SINS AGAINST YOU
Part 4

When someone's sin hits you like a stone, hurting you, there are four things you can do. The final option—Forgive. You don't have to forget, but God calls you to forgive.

What exactly is forgiveness? It's the daily choice to let the stone alone. You don't forgive once and for all any more than you make the choice to be patient once and for all. No, that stone is always there at your feet, which means every day, every moment, with every trigger, every memory, you have to make a choice to let the stone alone. To trust that God will take care of the justice. To believe that God knows what happened and his path, free from bitterness and vengeance, is the best way to be healed.

Once your hands are free of their sins, they are open to pray, to bless, and to reach out in reconciliation. Peter wrote, **"Repay evil with blessing, because to this you were called so that you may inherit a blessing"** (1 Peter 3:9).

I think I know where Peter learned that from. Jesus didn't repay us for our evil but instead blessed us by his blood. His calling was to love us, forgive us, and save us. His choice to let all of our sinful stones alone means that we have an inheritance in heaven.

I know forgiveness can feel impossible. So fix your eyes on the cross, where God makes the constant choice to let those stones alone, to forgive you.

MORE ON THE TOPIC . . .

"*Forgive* is a complicated word that's often misunderstood, so let me give you my simplest definition. To me, the word *forgive* simply means this: The daily choice to let the stone alone. I carefully crafted every word in that sentence. I called forgiveness a daily choice. It's not a feeling; it's not something that one day the light switch goes and you suddenly feel great about it. No, it's a choice that you make not once but every single day. People often get this wrong; they say, 'But, Pastor, I'm not sure if I have forgiven him.' *Have forgiven?* No, it's not a one-time thing. The question isn't: Have you forgiven him? The question is: Are you forgiving him? Today? You know, every day after that stone hits—boom—there it is. And tomorrow the stone's going to be there. And even if I throw it because that's the way the heart works, the stone is still going to be there. So forgiveness is the spiritual battle that we fight with the help of God to just let it alone. I know it happened; maybe I can't forget about it, but it's not my job. It's God's job to take care of the justice. It's the authority's job to take care of the consequences. Today I'm making the choice for the glory of God and for the good of my soul to let the stone alone."

From *Time of Grace* series *Forgiveness Is Offensive*, episode: "You Must Forgive EVERY Day"

DIG DEEPER

Have you ever thought about forgiving others as a choice—a choice to let that stone alone? What would that look like for you?

Which bothers you more emotionally—the sins that others have committed against you or the sins you've committed against God? Be honest. Explain your answer.

Read Romans 12:18. What does Paul urge you to do in order to restore any broken relationships in your life?

How do you do that? Read the rest of Romans chapter 12 and jot down some ideas here.

Jesus didn't repay us for our sins against him. Instead, list the blessings that he gives you each day.

What stones were thrown at you today?

How did you handle those stones?

Write a prayer of thanks. Thanks to Jesus for being so humble that he chose the cross for you. So loving that he loved his enemies. So committed that he didn't just forgive you; he reconciled you to God! He did everything possible to live at peace with you forever and ever. Amen!

When [Jesus] suffered, he made no threats. . . .
"He himself bore our sins" in his body on the cross.

1 PETER 2:23,24

WHAT TO DO WHEN SOMEONE SINS AGAINST YOU
Part 5

In 2018 Botham Jean was sitting in his own apartment when the unthinkable happened. Amber Guyger, a police officer, entered the apartment, mistakingly believing it was her own and assuming Botham was a burglar. She shot him, ending his life. Thirteen months later, when Guyger was sentenced to ten years in prison, Botham's brother, Brandt, took the witness stand to speak: "I hope you go to God with all the guilt. . . . I forgive you. I love you just like anyone else."

Brandt then asked the judge, "Can I give her a hug?" Once granted, he met Amber in the middle of the courtroom. She collapsed into his arms, and he embraced her for an entire minute (!) and spoke words of forgiveness into her ear.

Such shocking grace shouldn't surprise you. After all, that's what the gospel says every day: **"When** [Jesus] **suffered, he made no threats. . . . 'He himself bore our sins' in his body on the cross"** (1 Peter 2:23,24). Jesus didn't threaten to get us back for our sins. Instead, he handed everything over to God and suffered so that we could be saved.

Then, on Easter morning, Jesus asked his Father, "Can I give them a hug?" Once granted, he leapt out of the grave and spoke grace into our ears, not just for a minute but for every minute of all eternity.

That's why we love Jesus. He forgives the worst of us and the worst in us!

MORE ON THE TOPIC . . .

"God says: He forgives you. Every single day because of the blood of Jesus, every one of those stones that you have thrown at God sits at the foot of the cross. Jesus Christ himself makes the daily choice not to touch it, not to look at it, not to hover his hand above it. No, his forgiveness for you is so great. . . . How blessed are we when every transgression is forgiven? He lets it alone, and not just that, when your sin is covered up, there's not this pile of stones for God to stare at. It's covered up by the blood of Jesus. . . . You're forgiven. As you struggle today to let that stone alone, you're forgiven. And if the dust and the dirt are still on your hands from yesterday, you're forgiven. So, friends, be kind and compassionate to one another, forgiving each other, just as in Christ God forgave you— because it will be so beautiful when you do."

From *Time of Grace* series *Forgiveness Is Offensive* episode: "You Must Forgive EVERY Day"

DIG DEEPER

Read 1 Peter 2:21–25 and list at least three things that make Jesus worthy of our worship.

Copy the Lord's Prayer here. Pray it each day in the upcoming week. Pause after each line that mentions forgiveness in order to confess your sins personally to the Father and to release the sins personally committed against you.

Meditate on every word of Romans 8:1. Rank the top two words that give you comfort and explain why.

Evaluate: If God could forgive King David (an adulterer), the apostle Peter (a Jesus denier), and the apostle Paul (a former killer of Christians), he must be able to forgive me.

What "stones" have hurt you the most in your life? Looking back, which of the four paths did you choose to take? Which path are you taking today?

What stones were thrown at you today?

How did you handle those stones?

Write a prayer to God to send the Holy Spirit to help you let go of deep wounds today and tomorrow and for days to come.

**A man who owed [the king] ten thousand
bags of gold was brought to him.**

MATTHEW 18:24

THE MATH OF FORGIVENESS

Here's a story that Jesus *almost* told—There was a man who owed a king 100 silver coins. The king, knowing the man couldn't pay the debt, smiled and said, "I forgive your debt, all 100 coins." The forgiven man left, ecstatic over the king's forgiveness . . . until he ran into a neighbor who also owed him 100 coins. He demanded payment. Unlike the king, however, there would be no forgiveness. When the king heard what the man had done, the man who had just been forgiven *that very amount*, he was furious.

Do you recognize that tale? It resembles a parable Jesus told. Except for one little detail. In Jesus' actual story, the first man wasn't forgiven just 100 silver coins but instead **"a man who owed** [the king] ***ten thousand bags of gold* was brought to him"** (Matthew 18:24). The debt was not silver but gold. Not 100 coins but 10,000 bags of coins. It's hard to perfectly crunch the numbers, but some scholars suggest that the man owed the king $7,000,000,000 and was owed around $12,000.

Why did Jesus choose those numbers? Perhaps he knew we could never truly forgive unless we realized how much we have been forgiven. Not a silver coin or two but billions of dollars, paid in full at the cross.

If you're holding on to bitterness toward someone, take some quiet time with Jesus. Think deeply about how often and how completely you have been forgiven. Then you'll be ready to forgive.

MORE ON THE TOPIC . . .

"When you look at Jesus' cross, how much forgiveness do you see? How many of your stones sit beneath his feet? Your honest answer matters. 'The one who has been forgiven little loves little.' That's what Jesus said. 'But the one who has been forgiven much . . . well, they know how to forgive.' . . . This is what Jesus did for us. God piled every one of your sins at the cross and then nailed down the hands of his Son so that not a single stone would be thrown. So that the King would let every stone alone. So that his hands would be open to pray, 'Father, forgive them!' So that despite the consequences, there would be no condemnation. Not for you. Not for anyone who trusts in Jesus."

From *Time of Grace* series *Forgiveness Is Offensive*, episode: "When Forgiveness Feels Impossible"

DIG DEEPER

How many of your stones sit at Jesus' feet? Think about that. How does that make you feel?

When you consider the stones that have been thrown at you this week, why does remembering the stones Jesus has left alone help you with compassion toward others?

As you look back at the sins you've committed against your God, don't focus on the guilt or the shame. God wants you to focus on his amazing forgiveness. Write about what his forgiveness means to you.

Do a Google search to find other Bible passages about forgiveness. Write a few down here. God is amazing!

What stones were thrown at you today?

How did you handle those stones?

Write a prayer that God opens your eyes to the amazing mercy he's shown to you so that you can go and show that same mercy to others.

Follow me!

JOHN 21:19

JESUS RECONCILES WITH REAL SINNERS

There's a difference between forgiveness and reconciliation. Forgiveness is when you make the daily choice not to get back at the person who sinned against you. But reconciliation goes a step further. It restores, reunites, and rejoins separated people. If you're like me, you know that forgiveness is hard but that reconciliation is even harder!

That's one more reason why I adore Jesus. After his friend Peter sinned against him, denying that he even knew who Jesus was (Luke 22:60), our Lord made sure to reconnect with Peter after the resurrection. **"Follow me!"** Jesus invited him, just as he had three years earlier, long before Peter's epic failure (John 21:19). It would have been pure grace for Jesus to forgive Peter and then end their friendship. But it was grace on top of grace (on top of grace!) for Jesus to welcome Peter back to the table and call him his follower and friend.

Isn't that wonderful? When you sin, even in embarrassing ways, Jesus does more than forgive you. He refuses to let you wander through life alone, forgiven but far from him. Instead, Jesus reconciles with you, draws you close, and assures you that you are still his follower and friend. While true reconciliation might be rare in our broken world, it is the promise that the gospel makes to you. Believe it and enjoy that promise today!

MORE ON THE TOPIC . . .

"The death of Jesus reconciles us to God, drawing us into his presence, into his sight, where he smiles and blesses and loves. Even sinners like us can say, 'GOD is here' because he doesn't just forgive. He loves us. This is what we are to imitate. Live at peace with everyone. Forgive and bless and serve and be another living, breathing example that sin doesn't have to separate us forever. Just like it didn't with Jesus."

From *Time of Grace* series *Forgiveness Is Offensive*, episode: "I Forgave. Now How Do I Heal?"

DIG DEEPER

Explain in your own words the difference between
forgiveness and reconciliation.

Jesus forgives us, and like Peter, he wants us to follow him. Isn't that amazing? No matter what we've done—we are to follow him. What does following Jesus look like in your life?

Why is it essential to love/serve the person who sinned against you before deciding if it is possible to reconcile with them?

If keeping godly boundaries is a struggle for you, read through the book of Proverbs over the next month or so. Note here the wisdom of keeping your distance from destructive people.

Read Mark 16:1–8. How does the resurrected Jesus prove that he longs to reconcile with real sinners?

What stones were thrown at you today?

How did you handle those stones?

Write a prayer for God to show you the way to reconciliation with someone in your life.

If it is possible, as far as it depends on you,
live at peace with everyone.

ROMANS 12:18

WHEN SIN TEARS PEOPLE APART

I find Paul's words to the Romans as challenging as they are beautiful: **"If it is possible, as far as it depends on you, live at peace with everyone"** (12:18). While it takes two people to live at peace, Paul urges us to do everything in our power to restore the relationships that sin has broken.

How do you do that? In Romans chapter 12, Paul points to a few vital truths. First, don't be proud. One percent of the time, like in cases of child abuse, sin is one-sided. But the other 99 percent of the time, two sinners are involved in the situation. *She escalated it . . . but I might have started it. He threw this massive stone in our marriage . . . but I threw a thousand small ones first.* Living at peace starts with humility, with owning our part and confessing, not excusing, our sin. So don't let your hurt take away your humility.

Second, love them. Bless those who persecute you. Rejoice when they celebrate. Overcome the evil they did by doing good. Use your hands, not to pick up the sinful stones they threw at you but to serve and love them. That might not guarantee healing, but it's God's best path forward.

Those steps remind me of Jesus. So humble that he chose a cross for us. So loving that he loved his enemies. So committed that he didn't just forgive us; he reconciled us to God! He did everything possible to live at peace with us forever and ever. Amen!

MORE ON THE TOPIC . . .

"Let's summarize Paul's teaching: Step 1—They sin. They hit you and hurt you. Step 2—You look to God. You remember how he let your seven billion stones alone. Step 3—You forgive. You make the daily choice to let the stone alone. Step 4—You love. You pray and bless and feed and serve the sinner, doing everything you can. Step 5—Y'all reconcile, if possible. If it's not possible or if they aren't willing to change, you pray. From a distance, you pray for God to change their heart and bless them."

**From *Time of Grace* series *Forgiveness Is Offensive,*
episode: "I Forgave. Now How Do I Heal?"**

DIG DEEPER

What does it mean to live at peace with everyone, even those who are hard to live at peace with?

If you're in a situation right now where you're having a hard time living at peace with someone, is it possible that you're being prideful? Can you evaluate the situation and write down your part in the conflict?

Instead of picking up stones to get back at someone, what does this devotion say you should do with your hands?

How can serving others be a step forward in strained relationships?

Read 2 Corinthians 5:17-19. Take some time to break these verses down, meditate on them, and write them in your own words here.

What stones were thrown at you today?

How did you handle those stones?

Write a prayer for a heart of forgiveness, for humility, and for the strength to live at peace with everyone.

FINAL THOUGHTS

I love how realistic the apostle Paul is. While teaching on sin, forgiveness, and reconciliation, he wrote, **"If it is possible, as far as it depends on you, live at peace with everyone"** (Romans 12:18). Paul is pushing us to do everything we can to reconcile with those who sin against us. But notice the phrase "if it is possible." Sometimes it isn't possible, in this life, to fix what sin has broken.

Think of what infidelity might do to a marriage. Even Jesus recognized that the damage could lead to divorce (Matthew 5:32). Or think of what gossip might do to a friendship. Solomon knew such sins might separate close friends who are no longer eager to share their deepest struggles and secrets (Proverbs 16:28).

That's important to know. While we strive to forgive everyone who sins against us (Luke 11:4), it might not be possible to reconcile every relationship. That doesn't mean we're bitter or vengeful. It simply recognizes there are other factors involved. It's like a runner after a car accident. She might not be able to sprint like before, despite the work of rehab.

Thankfully, however, Jesus' forgiveness is perfect. Because of the cross, living at peace with God is always possible, no matter how ugly the sin or long-lasting the consequences. While we might struggle to trust the people who've hurt us, we can always trust that Jesus has helped us, giving us a perfect relationship with our Father. No distance. No separation. Just God with us until the day we see him face-to-face.

God is with you as you seek to forgive others!

Please note: If you'd like more on the topic of forgiveness or to watch the entire *Forgiveness Is Offensive* series, go to timeofgrace.org or the Time of Grace YouTube channel.

ABOUT THE WRITER

Pastor Mike Novotny has served God's people in full-time ministry since 2007 in Madison and, most recently, at The CORE in Appleton, Wisconsin. He also serves as the lead speaker for Time of Grace, where he shares the good news about Jesus through television, print, and online platforms. Mike loves seeing people grasp the depth of God's amazing grace and unstoppable mercy. His wife continues to love him (despite plenty of reasons not to), and his two daughters open his eyes to the love of God for every Christian. When not talking about Jesus or dating his wife/girls, Mike loves playing soccer, running, and reading.

ABOUT TIME OF GRACE

Time of Grace is an independent, donor-funded ministry that connects people to God's grace—his love, glory, and power—so they realize the temporary things of life don't satisfy. What brings satisfaction is knowing that because Jesus lived, died, and rose for all of us, we have access to the eternal God—right now and forever.

To discover more, please visit timeofgrace.org or call 800.661.3311.

HELP SHARE GOD'S MESSAGE OF GRACE!

Every gift you give helps Time of Grace reach people around the world with the good news of Jesus. Your generosity and prayer support take the gospel of grace to others through our ministry outreach and help them experience a satisfied life as they see God all around them.

Give today at timeofgrace.org/give or by calling 800.661.3311.

Thank you!